To Barbara Green-Love

Love Hope & Blessings
Bettye Stevens Coney
July 31, 1999

My
Soul Speaks Truth

Poetic Communication
by
Bettye Stevens Coney

My Soul Speaks Truth

Copyright © 1996 by Bettye Stevens Coney
Printed in the United States of America
ISBN 0-9648337-0-0

Library of Congress Catalog Card Number 96-67292

STEBRECO

All rights reserved. No part of this book may be reproduced in any form or by any means, electronic or mechanical, including photocopying without written permission from the author. All inquiries should be addressed to:

STEBRECO
Bettye Stevens Coney
P. O. Box 49-1058
Leesburg, Florida 34749

Art Work by
Arthur L. Dawson ETHNIC VISIONS
P. O. Box 680952 Orlando, Florida 32868

Printed by
Lawton Printers
185 Anchor Road Orlando, Florida 32707

Photos by
Steve Davis Photography
126 South 5th Street
Leesburg, Florida 34748

BIOGRAPHICAL SKETCH
OF
BETTYE STEVENS CONEY

Bettye Stevens Coney retired as an elementary school principal in June, 1995. Concurrent with her retirement, she received the Principal of the Year Award - Lake County Public Schools for her innovativeness in working with students at Rimes Elementary School in Leesburg, Florida. As an educator, she has served as music teacher, speech/language/hearing pathologist, Content Specialist for Speech Language Hearing Programs, dean, and assistant principal.

Her forte is communication. Regardless of its form, whether it's speaking, writing or singing, Bettye has the innate ability to touch one's heart and soul immensely. She states that she does not ever remember being unable to express herself. She remembers one of her elementary teachers being impressed by the content of a compound sentence which she turned in one day. The teacher questioned where she had gotten it.

Bettye has a gift for interacting with people. Give her an audience and she is most comfortable and in control. She is a people person and has always been a keen observer of man's inhumanity to man. She's known to speak out about her strong convictions regarding the well-being of others.

An unselfish, warm and caring character has enabled Bettye to be the recipient of such awards as Who's Who In American Education, Professional Leadership, Leadership Lake County, Woman of the Year, Phi Delta Kappa and numerous school, community and church awards. She has also hosted Black History radio talk shows.

Bettye is a graduate of Florida A and M University in Tallahassee, receiving a BS in Music Education. From the University of South Florida, she earned a Masters in Speech Pathology and through the University of Florida and the University of Central Florida she became certified in Supervision and Administration.

Bettye Coney resides in Leesburg, Florida with her husband, L. C. Coney. They have two daughters, Melodi and Gessner.

FOREWORD

The Soul does not lie. It shares an accord with truth that we should draw on in our journeys through life.

Bettye Stevens Coney, Florida educator, parent and civic leader, knows this. Her first book of poetry is aptly titled, <u>My</u> <u>Soul</u> <u>Speaks</u> <u>Truth</u>.

And indeed it does.

Coney takes the reader on a sojourn that chronicles the pang of racism and the jubilation in perseverance; the need for black self-redemption and the path toward that restoration; the rage of isolation that's calmed through belief in a Higher Being.

Undoubtedly, Coney's writing will strike a chord with African Americans. Her trials and tribulations are synonymous with black folk - the black experience, if you will.

Here she lends a poetic touch to stories that have been told in beauty salons, barber shops and church pews for centuries.

But there's more here than an affirmation for Black Americans.

There's also a message for White America, too. There is no need to read between the lines, for there is nothing to interpret.

Coney's poetry is straightforward:

She wants people - all races of people - to see life the way she sees, feels and understands it. So she recalls the bitter memory of being turned away from a segregated deli, the loneliness felt when her ability is needlessly questioned all because of her skin color.

So listen to this proud black woman.

Enjoy her undying but occasionally weakened spirit. There's something in these poems for everyone, especially since they emanate from the soul.

Rick Badie, Journalist
Orlando Sentinel Newspaper

INTRODUCTION

STOP WORLD! Listen to what I have to say for a change! As an African American, I AM EXHAUSTED! I AM FED UP AND I AM PUT OUT WITH READING AND HEARING PARTIAL TRUTHS (or no recognition of the truth at all) ABOUT SOME OF LIFE'S ISSUES. It is only I, or other people like me, who can express the TRUTH about the misery of being dehumanized, belittled, chastised, walked over, and looked over in our American society. As African Americans, evolving into the Twenty-first Century in America, we still find ourselves being repeatedly overwhelmed by sullen remarks and trying conditions, either at the work place, the market place, or other public places.

Furthermore, too few books, which illuminate the facts, fundamental thoughts, and feelings of the African American, are written and placed on public bookstore shelves. Too few African Americans are willing to take the risk to communicate THE TRUTH about ourselves, our convictions, and our relationships in society. Yet we continue to bear pain and hurt and suffer humiliation and depression because of numerous missing links of understanding - between African American and other cultures, as well as between ourselves and our race, and between ourselves and our Supreme Being.

The counteragent for lack of understanding and misconception is simple - COMMUNICATION! How will anyone ever know that I have an ache until I tell them? I AM READY TO TELL YOU OF MY ACHES NOW!

<u>My Soul Speaks Truth</u> is a book which communicates the aches, pains, and joys of relationships, the positive rewards of motivation, and the fulfillment of reaching the aspirations necessary for achieving in today's world. I express these truths in poetic form. I call it "Poetic Communication".

As an African American female, living in the Southern United States, it is my intent to share some of my experiences and insights, concerning a wide spectrum of subjects — discrimination, discord, disappointment, satisfaction, motivation, current issues, and relationships.

Ultimately, it is my profound hope that Black, White, Brown, Red, and Yellow people will be able to see, feel and understand as I have seen, felt, and understood the world in which I live.

TRUTH, through communication, is the only viable means left for African Americans to convey our courageous plight on the ever spiraling journey in pursuit of dignity for all.

DEDICATION

TO: My Beloved Mama and Daddy

    This book is dedicated to you with all of my love and much more. You were always by my side to lift me up and encourage me each step along the way. The examples you've set are the precepts by which I live today. Now that you're in Heaven, I just know that you're prompting God for even more of His best for me.

    I miss you so much!

                                      Loving you more each day,

                                      Your daughter,

                                      Bettye

FOR MY FAMILY

TO: My Loving Husband, L. C.

    Thanks, Honey, for always being there and supporting me in all my endeavors. It is because of the SUPER man that you are that you have never deterred me from being "my own person". Without your shoulder to lean on when the going was tough, life would have been even tougher. You're one in a million.

TO: My Darling Daughter, Melodi

    You've always been Mama's lead cheerleader. I appreciate all of your encouragement, boasting, and confidence in my abilities. You'll always be a sparkle of joy and fulfillment in my life. You're what God had in mind when he breathed breath into daughters.

TO: Step-Children, Aunts, Cousins, and In-Loves

    Step Children - You've shown your love to me, too,
        Thanks for all you do.

    Aunts - You become more endearing to me each day.
        Mama and Daddy would want it that way.

    Cousins - You're my sisters and brothers of which I haven't any - Thanks for sharing your love with me - plenty.

    In-Loves - We've made two families into one.
        The love we share is second to none.

        Love you,

        Bettye

VERY SPECIAL ACKNOWLEDGMENT

TO: My Dear Friend, Ms. Juanita Jones

My first book would have been nearly impossible without you.

Thank you so very, very much for your many long hours of expertise exhibited in coaching me - correcting my breathing (editing and typing) while I was impregnated with material for my book - from the first labor pains, through birthing the baby (producing the completed manuscript).

FOR HONORED INSIGHT

TO the Renowned: Susan L. Taylor
                   Editor In Chief
                   Essence Magazine

Without your wisdom and insight, I would still be at first base with my work.

Thank you for your unselfish and caring spirit. Truly, <u>IN THE SPIRIT</u> epitomizes the <u>ESSENCE</u> of you!

ACKNOWLEDGMENTS

My grateful appreciation is extended to the many who have touched my life in even the smallest way. My love and best wishes I give to you.

COMMUNICATION ENTRIES

Level I ....Dignity Not For Sale
Prelude
Why
Restless Inside
I Am What I Am
Be Your Own Person

Level II ....Hoops, Hurdles and Broad Jumps
Prelude
The Challenge
Wait A Minute
Unacceptance and Unaware
Let's Sort It All Out
Down Moments
Can't Make You See
Questions

Level III ....African American Men, Women and Youth
Prelude
The Black Man's Cry
The Black Man's Perseverance
Will the Right Black Man Step Forward
Wake Up Call to Black Men
Don't Call Yo'self No Daddy, No Mo'
Understanding the Black Man
I Am the Strong Black Woman
Women, Stand By Your Man
Egos
Black Youth of America
Transcending Difficulties (The Going Somewhere Train)

Level IV ....Situation America
Prelude
Back Then
Telling It Like It Is
Ku Klux Klan Rides Tonight!
The Meeting Room
Will America Lose Its Steam (over Affirmative Action)
Biases
We Ain' Crazy, White Folks
The Black Test
Black Woman's Madness
Judgments, Yardsticks and Measures
Lemme As' Y'all Som'n

Level IV, continued
A Black Child's Plea (Please, Help Me)
Tell Them
Sad
Wake Up, America, Wake Up!
Taking Applications (to Join the Rainbow Race)
Genuine Kindness

Level V . . . . .Come Fly with Me
Prelude
Sharing to Be Free
But, Why Can't I?
Mind over Fear
Self-Motivation
Ever Wonder How It Happens to Be The Neutral Race
Come on, Sister Girl!

Level VI . . . . .Loving
Prelude
Family
Talking with Uncle Essie
Visiting up Home
Beautiful People
My Baby Girl
When She Was Born
She's Daddy's Delight
To Her Loveliness
Hey! Little Red Head Girl
Only Children
    (An only Child)
There's A Little Church I Know
(New Bethel A. M. E., Okahumpka, Florida)
My Man and His Sax
From the Principal
(Referring to Teachers and Students at Rimes Elementary School)
True Friends Are
I Remember the Days
I Love Laughing

Level VII . . . . .The Holy Spirit Within
Prelude
My Supernatural Friend
    (The Holy Spirit Within)
Awesome, Powerfully Awesome
He Shows Me He's There
Magnificently Wonderful

Commentary

SHARING TO BE FREE

The mind within
Is mighty strong indeed-
Impulses no longer to wait
Nor thoughts that I care to impede.

Emotions - stored on the shelf of time-
Talents, gifts and experiences
Anxiously pausing in line.

Now I know why, for years, I've cringed, cried And sighed-
Simply because, I realize now, there's more, Much more of me inside.

Though numerous times I've wondered
What else He's ordained for me -
Now, believing the time has come
I see - it is more of my inner self I must
Share - to be free.

Whether it's a song to sing
A poem to pin -
Or a heart to cheer, and try to win

Of all these things
That are part of me -
I must share them totally - totally
. . . to be free.

LEVEL I

DIGNITY NOT FOR SALE

DIGNITY NOT FOR SALE

Precious are my Black roots. Even more precious was the loving, rich, nurturing, and positive family environment in which I grew up.

Mama and Daddy were God-fearing, hard working, soft spoken parents. As an only child growing up, my parents managed to provide for me all of my needs and most of the things that I wanted. In the eyes of the world, we were poor people. We lived in a wooden, tin top, three room house. (Mama contracted with the rent man to add a room for me.) BUT we were so, so, so rich in love, positive spirit, hope, and faith. Mama said I could become anything I wanted to if I believed and worked hard enough. From this precept I developed the "I can do it" mind that has always provided me with the "ump" I need to help circumvent the negatives I find in my pathway.

My family's love, as demonstrated by their actions, told me that I was someone very dear and special, equipped my soul, mind, spirit and body with the "stuff" necessary to endure the trials in my life.

This is why I proclaim - DIGNITY NOT FOR SALE.

Bettye Stevens Coney

WHY?

At the door, I stood
and on the handle, I placed my hand.
Inside, I thought I'd go
for lunch - a sandwich, salad or so.

But, no!
Their actions loudly exclaimed
for they who were inside,
as though causing no human pain,
locked the door and turned their backs.

From the handle of the door, my hand fell,
from their property,
I bewilderingly left
to go back and tell
what a day it had been -
a day of dehumanizing,
downtown hell.

To my surprise I soon learned
that one of the persons inside
was the postman,
who confessed,
the other's actions were not his style.

It was only because
I just happened to have appeared
in one of the many beautiful shades of black
that I was refused
and turned back.
But it's me
in technicolor.
Why should they have feared?

Dressed properly,
I certainly was in line.
As a matter of fact,
I was dressed sort of fine.

WHY?, Page 2

Oh, I know
it was
only because
the time had not come
for Blacks and Whites
together to enter the same door.

Instead,
it was for me
a locked front door
only because
the Civil Rights movement, they preferred to ignore.
And respect for the dignity and worth
of all mankind
wore faintly, if at all,
on their mind.

But their unkindness
only challenged us to seek change.
So we tread forward,
marching
Though sometimes the cadence became weak
and sluggish.
Yet, we marched
forward
hoping to catch up.

And, today,
it's only because many innocent people
(of the same color as I)
in all walks of life, gave their lives
for the fight for freedom that we proudly say:
"You may stifle my spirit for a short moment,
but you shall never suppress my soul;
for it is my soul which sustains me
because
my soul speaks truth.

Though I stand
without bitterness, the pain endures.
Though change continues and good deeds allure,
yet that moment is forever engraved in my mind.
Why wouldn't everyone want to be
genuinely kind?

Bettye Stevens Coney

RESTLESS INSIDE

I wish I could tell you why
Something inside of me
Could never completely comply
To all the things
They said I could
Or couldn't do
Because of the color of my skin.
Such projections made me restless,
Restless within.

I have always thought
Myself someone
Whom Mama said
Was Smart.
"You've got what it takes.
You're made from good stock."
Mama said I had to work hard.
"Work hard, child,
From beginning to start."

I wish I could tell you why
Something inside of me
Always said, "No".
Even though
The sign read, "Colored",
up top the door.

I wish I could tell you why
Something inside of me
Keeps pushing me forward,
Prompting me
To step outside of myself.
Something inside of me
Continues to stir, making me
Restless Inside.

Could it be
That He
Expects more from me?

I AM WHAT I AM

What I've seen
And what I've lived,
The pain I bore,
And the intimidation I wore
Was no issue for those who professed to know more.

What I've known
Is not always what I've shown,
But what I sense from down in my soul
Is what some people are about
And how they fit into an all too common mold.

What I've known
Is that in confidence my self-esteem rests
Because inside myself I always believe
That I can withstand any of life's tests.

I know that it's imperative
For me to know who I am and whose I am
If I am ever to reach my greatest ambition
And make a worthy contribution.

It is crucial for me
To remember from whence I've come,
And yet be focused enough
To know where I am going.

You may not choose to know me,
But, you see, it is because I know
Who I am
That,
I am what I am.

Bettye Stevens Coney

BE YOUR OWN PERSON

Be your own person.
No matter what comes or goes,
You must know who you are,
And not be changed by every wind that blows.

First seek the divine guidance you need
Then trust yourself to act.
Do the best that you can do,
And not what someone else declares for you.

Be your own person,
You'll feel better about yourself, indeed.
Come to the realization
That it's yourself you must please.

Get used to the feeling that
Sometimes you may have to stand alone,
But, if you're right, it's far more profitable
To stand alone
Than stand with the crowd that's wrong.

Be your own person.
It's the noble thing to do.
It may not make you popular,
But it's a priceless virtue.

LEVEL II

HOOPS, HURDLES AND BROAD JUMPS

HOOPS, HURDLES AND BROAD JUMPS

Being a double minority - Black and female, and living in the South, obtaining professional promotions in education did not come easy for me... not by any stretch of the imagination. But hard work, dedication and work ethics never did hurt anyone. It's a record that I am very proud of, and the lessons I have learned in perseverance act as historical reminders of my inner strength - a will to always be a productive entity in the organization, regardless of adversities. This will is so strong that it continues to prompt me never to give up because Mama told me, "Where there is a will, there is a way."

The hoops and hurdles that we sometimes have to promenade through only prepare us for bigger broad jumps for success in our lives.

Now one may say that your job tests, Mr. and Ms. Black Person, are no more trying than anyone else's. All of us work hard, so what's your point? TRUTH is, when you are BLACK, you just know you have a double dose of, let's say, self-proving to fulfill. The wisdom of our mamas and daddies taught us that principle. Were they wrong?

Bettye Stevens Coney

THE CHALLENGE

When at first
I entered your space,
Exhilarated were my feelings inside,
But you were cold.
Such emotions you couldn't hide.
And again
for the hundredth time
I'd have to prove myself to win.
"Why was there a battle raging?"
I asked myself within.
It was my pleasure -
the position I'd been assigned.
What pain and mental anguish you cause
by what you never say.
But actions speak all.
Don't put me through
this silly game you play.
I know what I'm doing;
just wait and you will see.
I will achieve the goal I am pursuing.
Nothing has ever been given to me
(on a silver platter).
I've always worked hard;
So what's the matter?
Despite my efforts, you oppose.
And though sometimes your blows
leave me gasping for breath,
challenges are
quite common to me now.
One thing for sure,
I'll insist of up front -
that's mutual respect.
It costs nothing, except
just common sense.

WAIT A MINUTE!

Now, wait a minute!
Wait one "cotton picking" minute!
Time out!
Let's regroup!
Conference time!
Between you and me
Put all the cards on the table
for me to see.
Your undercover plotting,
deceptive contriving,
and small group persecution
Is not a part
of your contract here.
What good
do your negative ways serve?
What growth
do they promote?
I insist
that I have your full support.
Listen to me closely.
This message you must note.
It's your constructive work
that I employ.
The organization cannot profit
from you pretenses and ploys.
I wish to empower everyone
who enters here
to use their initiative
I'll not interfere.
But, remember this:
Work for the good of all
Think big, act big,
not small.

Bettye Stevens Coney

UNACCEPTANCE AND UNAWARE

If I deserve a bum rap,
then give it to me.
If I don't deserve your respect and support,
then at least accept me as I am.

I beg you not to patronize me
because of the situation in which
we have been placed; (or the way fate is stacked)
I only ask that you not stab me in the back.

What is there about me
that makes you not accept me?
What is there about you
that causes you to dig ditches for me?

The time has long since come
for you to see that the result of my actions say:

I am intelligent.
I am talented.
I am free.
I am beautiful.
I am warm and caring.
I am fair and just.
I am giving.
I am love.

LET'S SORT IT ALL OUT

Let's sort it all out
I sense that you believe
That I am operating on your turf.
But, I've been assigned here.
Isn't that enough?

Yes. I will inherently show
That resistant side of me,
Strong and Black,
But never vindictive.
That's not my knack.

Have you been surprised
That I get the job done?
Even in the midst of your deceit,
I will rise above
And will not give in to defeat.

I see and understand who you are
I have read your actions many times.
But I refuse to let you get the best of me.
You're still dealing with the past
And how it used to be.

Let's sort it all out.
I'm in charge. You're not.

Bettye Stevens Coney

DOWN MOMENTS

I feel down;
I feel disgust -
Don't want nobody around.
I'll sort it out, I must.

I feel unappreciated;
I feel unloved -
Good will seems belated.
I need help from above.

I feel misunderstood, and so I cry.
Pain eases, but not for good.
I wonder why.

But I shall rise;
I'm destined to win;
I'll earn the prize.
You'll see, My Friend.

CAN'T MAKE YOU SEE

I've tried so hard,
Can't make you see
Your insight is marred
By your perception of me.

I've tried so hard,
Can't make you see
Our integrity we must guard
So our conscience is free.

I've tried so hard,
Just can't make you see
I'm not your enemy.
Try looking at yourself, inwardly.

Bettye Stevens Coney

QUESTIONS

Why do you tell me I can't when
I believe I can?
Why do you find fault with me when
I'm trying hard to please?
Why do you give me Epsom salts when
it's sugar I really need?
Why do you hurt my feelings when
it's you I want to please?
Why do you belittle me
when it's your approval I seek?
Why is your character so tough, so strong
and it is I you want to be meek?
Why do you just sit there when
I need your touch and your care?
Why do you not help me when
I sit lonely, in despair?
Why can't you hear me when
my silent voice rages in your ear?
Why don't you trust my vision when
I've never given you reason for doubt?
Why don't you go with me
rather than send me alone?
Why don't you humor me
and not speak to me in that tone?
Why don't you seek to know me
as I know you within?
Is it because I am a strong, but caring woman,
who threatens you with my determination?
Is it because I'm only a child
whose voice is not as strong as yours.
Is it because I'm the elderly
whose weakness frightens you?
Is it because I'm a man
whose influence intimidates you.
Is it because I'm different than you
and you question my good faith intentions?
Is it because I care about you
and you're content just as you are?
Tell me, why?

LEVEL III

AFRICAN AMERICAN MEN, WOMEN AND YOUTH

AFRICAN AMERICAN MEN, WOMEN AND YOUTH

My Soul Speaks Truth speaks TRUTH to us, as African Americans, as well as our white counterparts. For it is TRUTH which illuminates our way, if we allow it to do so. And, as is biblically stated, "it will set us free."

Each of us has probably experienced instances where the proverbial "Crab" (another brother or sister) tries to pull our toes in one way or another when he or she thinks we may be crawling upward and out of the barrel of complacency. They say we have been programmed that way since slavery, in order to keep us fighting among ourselves. If that is true... Damn! Mr. White Man, you did a good job!

I will not belabor the issue of the white man's programming us to act like crabs because it will appear to be making excuses for our escapades of shortsightedness. TRUTH is, we are very intelligent people; so when logical reasoning uncovers who one of the culprits is in our human dilemma as Black folks, then we must cease to commit that act of treason against ourselves - once and for all.

But there still remains the obstacles of inequity we face as Black people, trying to come up from the dungeon of not very far, aspiring to reach Avenue Success in our American society.

In this vein, I view our Black males most often being shafted in the work place, being put on the back burner of the stove for job mobility, and seldom being in the fast track for promotions. And there they sit - just toasting away - until many times they crumble.

At the other end of the spectrum, there are some of our young men who are incarcerated, some on drugs, and some who father babies and will not provide for their needs. Yes. We must find ways to end this terrifying nightmare.

I dare not omit mentioning the backbone, the power source and the "hold-it-togetherness" of the Black woman in our society. It has been her intelligence, fortitude, strength, and "with-it-ness" that has been one of the dominating forces that has helped to sustain our existence as Black people and as a nation.

Inherently, we bring with us these rich, productive qualities to the work place and wherever we are. But racial denial has kept and continues to keep too many of us waiting in the corridors of ugly prejudices. WHAT A WASTE, AMERICA!

Then, we have our able, talented, intelligent, and sometimes frightened children - OUR YOUTH. Not nearly enough positive commentaries are being made about the many who bite the bullets of life's entanglements and become successful role models for others to emulate.

But I remain hopeful. As a race which has survived many battles before, I submit to you that "we cannot give up. We must not give up!"

You and I have the power within our means to help another find his or her way.

Will you REACH OUT Today?

THE BLACK MAN'S CRY

You told him to prepare
for the challenges ahead.
He did as you directed;
Still he sleeps in limbo's bed.

You say to him, "Be patient."
"How long?" he asks. "How long?"
"Take a number at the end,
That way you won't go wrong."

Well wishers encourage him,
"Don't give up nor give in.
With endurance you'll make it.
I've been there, too, My Friend."

Bettye Stevens Coney

THE BLACK MAN'S PERSEVERANCE

History has neglected you
Amid the pages of time
Yet with perseverance you stand
Strong in body and mind.

The world will never know
The treasure that you are
With bits and pieces from the past
We proudly salute you:
Black man, Black Superstar.

You so boldly speak in silence
of your agony within.
How I admire your resilience
Your endurance unto the end.

Today is a new day,
We see.
Today is a new day,
They say.

But those who see
Will seldom say,
And those who say
Pay as they pass this way.

Sometimes your dignity
You let slide,
Still you persevere
With strength from inside.

The Black Man's Perseverance, Page 2

Sometimes your words
You silently keep.
Still you persevere
The harvest to reap.

Sometimes your self-esteem
Lowers and wears thin,
Still you persevere.
Determined to win.

May we stop today
And say a prayer
For our Black men,
To show them we care.

Cherished Black men,
We stand by your side;
Keep a steady pace,
Let peace abide.

Refuse to give in
To the test of time.
Dare to reach your destiny
in style sublime.

Bettye Stevens Coney

WILL THE RIGHT BLACK MAN PLEASE STEP FORWARD

Scarce are our Black men.
So scarce I could cry.
"Here's one here, Sir."
"No. He's proud and fly."

Go search the nation over;
Bring him back for hire.
"Here he is, Sir."
"Um - He's not my desire."

Look in foreign countries;
Surely there's one there.
"Here he is, Sir."
"No. His skin's too fair."

Call up Saint Peter;
He's waiting for your call.
"Here's what you ordered, Sir."
"No. He's too gray and bald."

WILL THE RIGHT BLACK MAN
PLEASE STEP FORWARD now.
You're wanted for hire
in the great by and by.

WAKE UP CALL TO BLACK MEN

Hello
My name is
Of course you know me
I MARRY you
I LOVE you
I MAKE love to you
And I have your babies, too.

I buy groceries and cook for you.
I work and buy clothes for you.
I wash and iron for you.
I balance the checkbook for you.
I clean and operate the house for you.
And I look good for you.

I listen to your war stories.
I listen to your work stories.
I listen to your family stories.
I listen to your ego stories.
I listen. I smile. I listen.

Why am I calling?
Well,
Huh.
THIS IS WHY I'M CALLING.
You know -
last Sunday when we were going to church,
you opened your door,
and left me standing beside my door,
while you got inside the car
and started the engine.
That must stop, Honey.
You see -
I've been doing some thinking
Seems like
I'm doing all the giving
while you enjoy all the living.

Bettye Stevens Coney

Wake Up Call to Black Men, Page 2

Wake up call!
These are the changes:
From now on, when we get ready to go,
first, open my door,
tuck the princess in
then we'll go.

The other day
inside the restaurant
you pulled out your chair
and sat down just as nice.
From now on, when you pull out chairs
it will be done twice.

When we walk down the street,
I can't control who we meet,
but before you turn your head
in the direction of another,
be darn sure you've said
to the woman you've wed,
"You sho' look fine,
Baby of mine."

And,
for no occasion at all,
I need to hear you say
sweet and caring words
in some romantic way.

Oh, yes,
as it has been said,
"Actions speak louder than words."
It's always alright
to show me
you love me,
any time,
day or night.

My Soul Speaks Truth

DON'T CALL YO'SELF NO DADDY, NO MO'

Food, clothing and shelter
Are basic human needs -
Your children must come first.
Did you your responsibility heed?

If the answer is no,
Don't say anything mo'.
Be a real man; get a job.
'Til ya do,
Don't call yo'self no Daddy, no mo'.

Real men love their children enough
To care enough
Rather than
Sitting around, thinking you're cool,
Playing tough.

Fella!
Ya ain't what the bird
Left on the fence (that's it),
And you're disgustingly absurd.
Haven't you any pride
under that supposedly
suave hide?

Now don' come gittin' mad wit' me!
'Cause I'm tellin' ya like it is.
Git a job
So your children's necessities
They no longer
From others rob.

When you get a job
And get your money,
Don' go 'round flashin' yo' money,
Tryin' to be big
And actin' like a nig'.
Be a man, Son.

Take da money tuh da chullin mamma.
'Til ya do,
Don' Call Yo'self No Daddy, No Mo'.

Bettye Stevens Coney

UNDERSTANDING THE BLACK MAN

Understanding the Black man
means understanding history.
Understanding history
produces a quality of understanding
about the reason for his actions
(though they are
very strongly
unpalatable today).

The Black man (only some of them)
appears to conduct himself,
in part,
as though there is still
some mystical force
which drives his unconscious mind
back,
back in time
to play out the resentment and hostility
of his early existence,
an existence which
he acts out with persistence,
an existence which seemingly will be ever present
and deeply etched in the recessive memory
of his mind,
causing him to be
elusive, passive, uncaring and
aesthetically blind.

That early existence
shall be recapitulated
through the visualization of slavery.
Remember?
Who was it
that was snatched away
from his family time and time again -
Never seeing his children grow up?
Never being part of a family?
Never knowing all of the children
that he'd fathered?
It was the Black man.

Understanding the Black Man, Page 2

He served as stockman for the plantation -
That was his job.
There was never a need for flirtation
with the women.
He was ordered,
"Make plenty babies."
His charge was to keep
the healthy, husky babies coming.

So he did,
insuring
that the slave master's work
would be done:
plowing, hoeing, planting, picking cotton
from sunrise to sundown.
Then
he was sold to another plantation
to "stock" those women
with babies
and to work the crops.

Therefore,
the Black man (only some of them)
never learned the lesson of responsibility,
never learned the language of emotions.
He never learned -
He never quite learned.

And such
was the inheritance of the Black man,
generation after generation.

But (you say)
those things happened
over two hundred years ago.
How (you ask)
could traits
possibly be
still deeply embedded in the recesses of the mind
of some Black men.

I don't know,
but aren't they so?

Bettye Stevens Coney

I AM THE STRONG BLACK WOMAN

I make no apologies
for myself and others
who by mere inheritance
have had to be strong and enduring.

I make no apologies
and I plead for no sympathy
because the plight for me
was ordained since slavery.

You see. I am the strong Black woman.
Let me tell you how that happens to be:

At the slave market,
I stood in the blazing hot sun.
My baby child clinched in my arms,
so close to my bosom, so close to me.

He was my seventh child
all that I had left.
I cried out to God in heaven above,
praying every word I could think of,
"Please, God, don't let them take him away."

I cried loudly with all my might.
With tears running down my cheeks, I cried.
But no one heard the desperate cry
that witnessed of the anguish within.

Then it happened again
I had to give him up to the slave master,
to grow up without his mama,
to grow up, facing unknown disaster.

I am the Strong Black Woman, Page 2

Now all my family is gone,
and all that's left to do is pray.
I pray to stay healthy and strong;
I pray to see my family again someday.

At the new place, I can't let them see
how I worry, yearning to be free.
And I must be quick to do as I am told.
I must be strong -I must not break that mold.

You see, I am the strong, Black woman -
Throughout my African American history
I have sustained myself with broken bits and pieces.
Even to myself, I am a mystery.

I am the strong Black woman -
I must succeed;
I must be strong,
setting examples for others to heed.

WOMEN, STAND BY YOUR MAN

Part I

Women, always stand by your man.
Lift him up
as often as you can.
Give him comfort
when life gets rough.
Understanding
that God lovingly made women
able to endure
and stand tough,
In the home,
he should be the king.
And, yes,
you should be his love,
his only fling.
When big decisions must be made,
help him to see all sides
rather than a narrow view,
making sure momentum isn't
lost or that he won't have to suffer
undue cost.
Women, always stand by your man.
You should be his number one fan;
love him
with all of your heart,
tenderly, passionately,
and from this message
never depart.

All Things Being Equal,
Stop Here.
When Things Are Not Equal,
Move to Part II.
This message Is the Sequel
for you:

Women, Stand by Your Man, Page 2

Part II

Now, Women,
read my lips.
Here are a few other tips:
If yo' man ain' treatin' ya right,
YOU KNOW WHAT I MEAN
. . . in his arms;
he ain' holdin' YOU tight;
ain' payin' no bills;
ain' givin' YOU no money,
'n' stayin' out late at night,

som'n' wrong som'wher'.
You need to see what goin' on dere.
I ain' advocatin' to you da be no fool.
Never let a man
drain ya of yo' pride
when he got other interest
OUTSIDE.
Pull yo'self dageth'r.
Fix yo'self up!
Git a foxy hai' do.
Buy you a dress or two.
Look ya very best.
Put HIM through the test.
Yo' man MAY be lazy,
But he SHO' ain' crazy!

If your man gets the message
and you work problems out,
fine!
Go back to Part I.
Forgive the hurt done
and Stand By Your Man.

If he doesn't get the message,
move to Part III.
But I leave that up to
you and Thee.

Bettye Stevens Coney

EGOS

Ladies, Gentlemen and Youth:
What I will say is the truth.
Let's have a fireside chat, please.
The message I hope you'll seize.

I graciously applaud you
for your self-esteem and pride.
They charm my spirit inside,
and
I am quick to recognize your intelligence.
That, of course, you can't hide.
I salute all of you, My People,
for your accomplishments - a HEAP!
But,
Brothers and Sisters!
Some of your egos you can KEEP!

Wait!
Don't turn me off just yet.
Here's the record I will set:
When we gather for a meeting
at the table we're all seated
to discuss a vital issue
usually
on what methods to pursue
to help Black folks like me and you,
may I suggest
that you patiently listen
to everyone's point of view,
including
what you have to say, too,
then, together reach a compromise
by producing a master plan,
depicting our thinking is wise,
showing that leaders care enough
to forget self and recognize
there's strength in unity of mind.
All our help is needed
to help save mankind.

Egos, Page 2

Rather than
becoming indignant and aloof
because YOUR way
was rejected that day.
When we meet
consensus must be our goal
in search of solutions
for the good of the whole.
It doesn't matter a bit
whose suggestions were picked
to get the job done in the end.
What does matter a lot
is that our objectives are met!

From the big to the little,
on every issue of life,
Black folks' perspective is crucial.
Let's have our say without strife.
No one needs to be reminded
of tasks confronting us now.
With our brilliance and might
we must find answers somehow.
I pray
somewhere along the way
we come to realize
that our total worth is indeed paralyzed
when we allow our egocentricity to preclude
our thought process,
thereby
negating
consensus of mind,
then, society's benefit becomes penalized

Now, I'm intending no hurt, blame or shame.
I'm merely presenting the truth
to ladies, gentlemen and youth.

Bettye Stevens Coney

BLACK YOUTH OF AMERICA

Listen up, Black Youth of America
These are some things you must know:
The lesson
you must learn,
(and I'll speak
my words loud and clear
for you to hear) -
You must never take for granted
anything that you see,
anything that you have,
nor anything that you enjoy-
Because
these things didn't just
happen to come
through some mystical act or ploy.
You see,
many men and women before you
had pride and dignity, too.
They risked their lives
and gave their hides
All
for fine
young people like you.
I'm talking about
men and women of impeccable substance,
African American men and women,
who dared
to think, act, and to do for themselves,
fighting their way
out of the muck and miry clay
and finding their way
to freedom
as we know it today.
You see,
the places you go
were not always open
to you
for your enrichment and entertainment.
The freedoms you enjoy
were paid for with a precious price.
The schools, restaurants, movies, and the beach,
even some churches years ago,
were out of your reach,
but today
such places are there
for you, too.

Black Youth of America, Page 2
But,
don't rest on your laurels,
Black Youth of America, thinking
you've got it made in the shade.
Such unrealistic reasoning
simply isn't true.
You've got your part to do:

If
you want to say
"Thank you"
for so many sacrifices
made on your behalf,
start now
by showing respect,
especially to your parents
and to all peoples
of every race, color, creed and kind,
whom you may find
in your pathway.
Keep your head on straight,
Girls and Guys.
our future depends on you.
Stay in school;
follow the golden rule
by doing unto others
as you would have them
do unto you

The choices and the challenges
are yours,
Black Youth of America.
Either
you take a negative, defeatist attitude,
and we suffer
your demise
or
you keep a positive mind and attitude,
and go for the prize
(you must).
Then
success you'll realize!

Bettye Stevens Coney

TRANSCENDING DIFFICULTIES
(The Going Somewhere Train)

So what if you're born poor -
Your daddy skipped town
and again to your house
he'll never enter the door.
Yes, I know. . .
Your Mama's on drugs;
You can't see your way out.
You, your brothers and sisters
look at your situation
in misery and doubt.

So what if you live in the apartments,
the Villages, the circle or quarters, too
You must enable yourself to see
beyond the shadow and around the tree.
You must always look for possibilities.

But what about
what people will say of you -
(the guys and the girls
with whom you have clout)?

Forget about your cronies
when a better life for themselves
they do not wish to make.
Wish them well
but with them, don't relate.

Go to someone you trust.
Pour out your troubles.
Cry if you must.
Just take a chance -on life.
Live by your sparkling dreams,
but not the dreaded knife.
Take a chance on life.
Go to a teacher, coach or pastor
Go to someone you trust,
someone whose ways
you want to master.

Just, please, don't throw your life away.
The world needs you
and what's contained in your brain.
Get on the right track now
and catch the "Going Somewhere Train."

LEVEL IV

SITUATION AMERICA

Arthur D.

SITUATION AMERICA

America is the sweetest land I know. Of course, it's home. And that's what home is all about - It's loving and caring about each other. Home is about teaching its young and seeing about its old. It's about each of its family members assuming responsibilities and being given opportunities to grow up and become contributing individuals in our communities.

I LOVE AMERICA - make no mistake about it. I love it just as I love my individual home.

America is also about EQUALITY, JUSTICE, AND DIGNITY for all. Here's where our conflicts lie. . . .

I need not enumerate for us what our problems are. I shall explain THE TRUTH about how BLACK AMERICANS, some of us, I suppose, view our situation in America.

For some, the tolerance of double standards, injustices, discrimination and sullen inhumane treatment has become an acceptable way of life. For others of us, who will never, ever accept man's inhumanity to man as just an intended way of life, we will always seek ways to communicate the presence of these injustices to the powers that be and to bring about change.

I firmly believe that open communication is the only viable means by which we can derive understanding about our misunderstood differences. Hence, through our understanding, we declare our similarities.

Then, and only then, shall we be able to move forward with unity - proclaiming PEACE, JUSTICE, EQUALITY and DIGNITY for all.

Until then this is <u>SITUATION</u> <u>AMERICA</u>.

Bettye Stevens Coney

BACK THEN

Growing up **BACK THEN**
in my little town
of Leesburg, Florida
everybody was caring,
protective and most
were nice to be around
BACK THEN
streets were all dirt and clay
Few people had indoor toilets,
sinks in the kitchen with running water
But we had electric lights though.
They'd set the whole place aglow,
showing cracks in walls
dull paint on ceilings, doors and all
Lights were hung
set dead center, ceiling top
with long string floating,
waving after you'd pulled it
or tugged it as with a pop
BACK THEN
everybody had an ice box
Ice man came once or twice a week
He'd deliver the ice, put it in the ice box
so our food we could keep
Tall tales were told
about the ice man
Whether they were true
I wouldn't know
Talking neighbors said
some tales were so
BACK THEN
the town was segregated
White people lived in their section
and we, "colored people",

Back Then, Page 2

lived in ours
White folks entered FRONT DOORS
while Black folks entered BACK DOORS
Black folks were expected to answer
YES, M'AM, NO, M'AM, YES, SIR, NO, SIR
work as we were told for sure
certainly no less, but Black folks
usually did more
BACK THEN
we attended separate schools
used discarded White folks books
as a rule
But that's all right
same information we attained
Covers of books didn't matter much
It was knowledge
we were in search
our teachers were smart, dedicated and witty
The subject matter we quickly learned
or, on our "hinies" they had no pity
BACK THEN
our high school band was the best
marched in downtown parades
always behind the horses
stepping over smelly mess
BACK THEN
we rode
in back of public transportation
'til Rosa Parks sat up front refused to move, causing boycotts
and White folks aggravation

Bettye Stevens Coney

Back Then, Page 3

BACK THEN
a dime would buy a strawberry soda
and a bag of potato chips
A nickel would buy a big boy, popsicle
package of cookies or five penny pieces of bubble gum
There was always enough to share
and give someone else some
BACK THEN
"doing the right thing"
was every family's honor and thrust
We strove to do good. It was a must! -
so the town's people
would think highly of us
Do good! Excel!
It was our pleasure
The family's name we upheld
BACK THEN
we went to town every Saturday
Butler's Parking Lot
is where the Black folks gathered
Everybody would visit, laugh and talk
going from car to car, we'd roam and walk
It was our weekly special treat
shopping at McCrory's and Vincent Dime Stores
Then at the Fain Theater, some of us would meet
BACK THEN
Sunday meant:
Sunday School, morning service
and night church, too
it was all part
of what we were expected to do
Those were the days
They've come and gone
Remembering when
is history now
But part of me will always be **BACK THEN**

TELLING IT LIKE IT IS

There should not be
any reasons why
HERE
IN AMERICA
AFRICAN AMERICANS
still fight for EQUALITY
JUSTICE
and DIGNITY.
It's Unbelievable
Inconceivable.
It's ludicrous
the Twenty-first Century
finds us
not very far
from plowing fields, hoeing the cotton
and cleaning Miss Ann's house
for one dollar and twenty-five cents
A WEEK.
African Americans
are still driving a horse and buggy to town
all meeting down behind the feed store
out of the reach and sight of other folks.
Conveniently
out of-sight, out of mind.
We are still standing out in the patch
of a hundred yesteryears
trying desperately hard to wave down
a jet rocket as it passes by.
There we stand
waving
waving a white handkerchief if you will.
Somebody promised us
over two hundred years ago
that we, African Americans,

Bettye Stevens Coney

"Telling It Like It Is", Page 2

would be on that jet rocket
certainly by the Twentieth Century.
Still we stand in the patch waving
waving our white handkerchief
Still we stand in the patch hoping
hoping to be noticed
Still we stand in the patch crying
crying to be heard.
Like the voice in the wilderness our echo
is our only feedback, our only response.
African Americans
are still being sold
as if in slavery
an unwanted bill of goods
while the slave master
continues to write and break
the laws of the land,
and they refuse to see each man
as an equal
refusing to allow
not much of the apple pie
to be enjoyed by those
who painfully work hard
and desire a taste
from the table of plenty.

For over three decades and more
we've been singing,
WE SHALL OVERCOME.
Yes
on that Great Gittin' up morning
Fare Thee Well,
Fare Thee Well.

THE KU KLUX KLAN RIDES TONIGHT!
(I'm Scared, Daddy)

"Daddy, what time will we
Pick up Mama from work tonight?
I'm scared, Daddy!
People say
The Ku Klux Klan Rides Tonight!
Wonder why, Daddy?
Did some colored folks do something
The white folks didn't like?
People say
They'll march down Pine Street,
Lake and Magnolia,
Maybe
Parker, Washington, Bisby,
Indiana and East Streets, too.
Bet nobody
Will be on our streets - tonight.

Will the Ku Klux Klan
March in the white neighborhood
Too, Daddy?
Wonder if their little girls
Are as scared as I am.
Bet they'll hide, too.

When we get in the car
To go pick up Mama from work
I'll just keep my head down
Way down
So they won't see me, Daddy.
But
You must be careful, Daddy.
I don't want those men with white sheets
To get you
'Cause we gotta go pick up Mama from work
And bring her home,
So we can lock up
And be safe tonight.

Bettye Stevens Coney

The Ku Klux Klan Rides Tonight! Page 2

>Daddy,
>Be sure to drive just right.
>I don't want the police to pick a fight
>'Cause we gotta go pick up Mama from work
>And bring her home,
>So we can lock up
>And be safe tonight.
>
>Is it time to go now Daddy? okay.
>I'm scared, Daddy!

THE MEETING ROOM

"You're saying the same thing
I said, Sir."
or, didn't you hear me?
Must I stand and scream?
Then you'll say
I'm loud, unladylike, uncouth.
Oh, I know,
I must be
the Biblical character, Ruth.

When will men ever learn
It's not always their turn
to speak and hog the show,
not hearing what others know?

Now you're saying,
"That's just like a woman. . . ."
You think I'm sensitive, paranoid
and very easily annoyed.

No.
What I am saying
is that
your superior ego
denotes insensitivity, shortsightedness
and more.
Look around you and see
your female counterpart
also
has her degree.
Now,
there's no offense intended.
We all must be intellectually
and socially
blended.

Bettye Stevens Coney

The Meeting Room, Page 2

        May I suggest to you
        Next time
        try switching the shoe -
        Pretend you're me
        and I'm you.
        Observe
        the meeting room dynamics -
        Are you
        the meeting room "know it all"?
        or
        Are you an "equal access" partner?
        and
        Shouldn't everyone
        "oughta"?

WILL AMERICA LOSE ITS STEAM
(over Affirmative Action)

Let's face facts, folks
Affirmative Action
means positive action.
Without Affirmative Action
America stands to lose
its diversity and big-hearted shoes.
Will America stoop that low
and refuse to grow
to the optimum level of its potential
by giving up its means
to equalize all our dreams?
At best,
we've only just begun
to run
an uphill race,
and we're traveling at a very slow pace.
The journey which we travel has rocky roads;
it has wooden bridges
with nails turned upward in its boards -
A journey where speed
nowhere correlates to the peoples' needs.

Like
The Little Red Engine that goes putt, putt, putt,
it's slow,
but
at least, we were moving forward,
though presently
we appear to be in a rut, rut, rut.
Will America Lose Its Steam
by eradicating Affirmative Action
thereby
negating, for some,
equal access to reach for a dream?

Bettye Stevens Coney

Will America Lose Its Steam, Page 2

Now many in mainstream America say,
"If you're qualified,
an equal job you'll get with equal pay,
and there's no need for Affirmative Action
that way."
Do ya'll think we crazy?
Ain't eb'n no point in tellin' dat lie no mo'.
As has been said
"If mama ain't in da kitchen
guardin' da cookie ja',
somebody go' steal da cookies.
....dat's fa sho"

It's not that every white person
is predicted to play the game unfairly,
but let's face the truth
Placing a Black person over a white person
happens
rarely.
Though their qualifications may be
the same or better,
it's a phenomenon we seldom see.

America,
I challenge you,
especially those who sit on the power pew,
to see the facts realistically
and to evaluate the numbers statistically,
then you will see
as do we
that the well-being of minorities
measures far too much lack;
and opportunities to compete
are under attack.

Will America Lose Its Steam
and allow The Little Red Engine
that goes putt, putt, putt
to eventually revert back
to the way it used to be,
keeping minorities in a rut, rut, rut?

BIASES

I am the Girl Friend
I am the Sister Girl
I am the Strong Woman
I am the Black Woman
I am the African American Female
Choose any of the list.
Misconceptions about me
put my character at risk.

When you compare me,
usually
to my white female counterpart,
you see things
most times
that I am not.
I just know that I'm equally as smart.
Then
you use negative terms
when defining
who I am.

When there is a need -
Yes, I will take over the situation
at hand, you call me bossy.
I am not!
You see -
I am a born leader.
In my culture,
most times, I've had to be the boss
or suffer the cost.

When I strongly project myself,
presenting my side and questioning yours,
you call me argumentative.
I am not!
You see -
I am competitive.
I am the business woman;
I am the single parent,
who has had to learn how
to recognize a bargain
in order to feed hungry mouths.

Bettye Stevens Coney

Biases, Page 2

When you see and hear me,
strongly telling the facts, pro and con,
usually with much expression,
you call me aggressive.
Yes. I am that.

You see
I am aggressively assertive
because nothing has come easy for me,
yet, I have learned to be strong.
I have been taught well.
Lessons I've learned
now others I can tell.

When you see me
ill tempered
because I may not understand
the rules by which
I am being judged this time,
You call me cranky.
I am not!
You see -
I am cautious
because I can't always trust you
to do by me
as you say you'll do.

When you hear me
reflecting from my insight,
calling things that are not
as though they are,
you call me
an idle dreamer.
I am not!
You see -
I am wise;
I have learned to trust God,
The Supreme Being in my life,
My Supernatural Provider,
My Source,
and Hope
for tomorrow!

My Soul Speaks Truth

WE AIN' CRAZY, WHITE FOLKS

We ain' crazy, White Folks
Naw ---------------- We ain' crazy
Naw. We ain' crazy!
Got good sense
Got plenty of 'em, too.

Now lemme tell y'all a thin' or two
'bout how y'all do.
'lection time come 'roun'
y'all start callin'
down in our town
wanna see what we thank
We be thank'n' all de time
We ain' jis' start thank'n'
'cause y'all run'n' fa one of dem positions
down der
Wher' y'all been at all befo'
We been right here
RIGHT 'chere'
And nobody come knockin' on our doo'
jis' wanna git our vote
Den don' thank 'bout us no mo'

We ain' crazy, White Folks
Naw ------------------- we ain' crazy
Naw, we aint crazy!
Got good sense
Got plenty of 'em, too

Sho be nice to kno' y'all care
all through de yea'
We got our concerns, too
We care 'bout holes in de road
drug dealers in de 'hood
ugly surroundin's
problem chullin, can' be understood
Wher' y'all at den?
Dat's right!
Ain' no 'lection to win
Won' y'all call us
fa some of dem close doo' meetin's
when y'all cussin' Niggertown

57

Bettye Stevens Coney

"We Ain' Crazy, White Folks, Page 2

Yeah, I said de "N" word
I SAID IT. I SAID IT!
Ain' go' bite my tongue now
y'all say it all de time
We say it, too!
But y'all bett' not let Us
hea' y'all say it
'cause we git uptight den -
wanna fight

An' don' come gittin'
all uppity wit' me
Girl Friend and Home Boy
Ya don' said Nigger befo', too
But it's private stock
'tween me and you, though
ain' it?
All over TV
dey be talkin' 'bout us
sayin' da "N" word
We kno' y'all talkin' 'bout us!
We smart nuf da kno'
"N" stand fo' Nigger
But y'all bett' not say it, though

We ain' crazy, White Folks
Naw ---------------- We ain' crazy
Naw. We ain' crazy!
Got good sense
Got plenty of 'em, too!

Den some mo' y'all got signs ya use
when ya wanna say de word
But don' say it -
Like waving ya hand
front ya face
or sayin' "one of dem"
We kno' who y'all be talkin' 'bout

We Ain' Crazy, White Folks, Page 3

    Jis' like
    y'all can' mistake us in a crowd
    (or one on one either)
    'cause we don' 'similate well
    in de mixin' pot
    y'all can' hide at all
    y'alls use of de word
    BE BETTER NO ONE SAID IT, NONE 'TOLL!

    We ain' crazy, White Folks
    Don' tol' y'all dat!
    we ain' crazy
    We ain' crazy!
    Got good sense
    Got plenty of 'em, too!

Bettye Stevens Coney

THE BLACK TEST

The Black Test -
What is it?
I will explain.
You see,
The Black Test
is difficult
for many of us to pass.
We can't see it,
but we know it's there.
We can't read it,
but we see its writing on the wall.
We can't study for it
because the variables are too many.
We can't order it on microfiche,
but we know it's finely printed
in the minds
of those who make decisions about our lives.
We can't request it from the library,
but we know
there are unwritten volumes in existence somewhere.
The Black Test -
Many people have applied,
but too few
have been allowed to pass that test.
Yes,
the color of the paper of the test
is white.
And yes,
the colors of the pens with which we write
are various hues.
And yes,
the answers to all of questions on the test
may be correct,
but
the test we have to take and pass
is a test like none other.
It is exclusively for African Americans.
It is
The Black Test.

BLACK WOMAN'S MADNESS

They overlooked ME
to say, "How do you do"
to Ms. Elizabeth Ann Pew,
While I sat there
just as BIG and BLACK as CAN BE
and way later
they said,
"OH! I didn't see you there."
I dare act as if I care!

First thing in the morning,
when someone I am meeting,
a request is made of me
BEFORE
the day's greeting!

In my culture
I have been taught
to be proud of who I am,
to rise to the occasion,
to dress - appropriately,
professionally,
and act accordingly.
So.
Don't look at me
cross-eyed
or pretend I'm not there
because of what I wear!
I take pride
in my job or position.
Check it out;
it's a Black tradition!

Bettye Stevens Coney

"Black Woman's Madness", Page 2

> A line has not be formed.
> Very near the cashier I stand,
> waiting to be helped.
> ... I'll be next
> anytime now -
> I think. At least, I hope.
> Still there I stand
> while my white counterpart,
> who arrived after I
> did is kindly served
> then departs.
> "WAIT A MINUTE, MISS,
> I'M NEXT. I INSIST!"
>
> HIS attention
> I am not seeking.
> To MY business
> I am attending.
> If YOUR man
> looks at me
> the glance I do not see.
> Don' git all mad wit' me.
> I don' wont YOUR man.
> Freeze, Girl Friend!
> I have my own man
> with whom I'm well pleased!
>
> "Hello,
> this is MR. NELSON.
> Let me speak to John."
> Pardon me, PLEASE,
> If you are MR. NELSON,
> likewise
> the MAN in MY family
> deserves equal respect.
> I RESENT this gross neglect!

"Black Woman's Madness", Paqe 3

"Colored folks
know how to dance, sing, run and hit a ball
Real Good"
True!
We are proud of all good things we do.

JUST DO NOT FORGET
AFRICAN AMERICANS
ALSO
HAVE FULLY DEVELOPED
BRAINS.
WE HAVE BEEN PROVING
THAT FACT
SINCE WE WERE CHAINED
AND BROUGHT
TO THIS COUNTRY OVER TWO HUNDRED YEARS AGO.
OUR BLOOD IS PART OF THE RIVERS THAT FLOW.
OUR BLOOD PROVIDED
THE RICHNESS FOR
AMERICA'S SOIL.
AMERICA WAS BUILT
BY SWEAT AND LABOR
AS OUR ANCESTORS TOILED.

OUR INTELLIGENCE
AND CREATIVE MINDS
ARE ETCHED IN
EVERY CORNER OF THIS NATION.

Don't treat me shabby
'cause my hair is nappy.
Treat me JUST
then I don't cause
a fuss!

Ignorance by some folks
is viewed with disgusting
sadness.
When stereotypical acts
are repeated,
they become
A BLACK WOMAN'S
MADNESS.

JUDGMENTS, YARDSTICKS AND MEASURES

Play the game by the rules -
We've all been taught to do.
I have no problem with that
When the game is fairly played -
It's true.

What's hard for me to digest
Is when there's one rule for you
And there're three for me to do.

Is it that you're unaware
That I can calculate, too -
All the times I have to prove
Myself competent for you?

When your judgment of me
Is stymied by the color of my skin
or, how wide I can stretch my lips to grin.
I have serious problems with that, my friend.

Let not stereotypical thinking
Be your yardstick for me.
I am as capable as many you see
And wiser than most.
No boast.

Let your judgment of me
Be not distorted by the sound of my speech
When I speak.

But rather,
Judge me by the depth of my words,
The integrity of my work
And the dignity of my character
These are the elements that matter.

The yardstick in life
Can be attained by all who enter in,
But keep the measures equal
In order for one to have a possible win.

My Soul Speaks Truth

LEMME AS' Y'ALL SOM'N'

Y'all eba notice dat a fact
don' become a whole fact
'til it's respected by my friend, a white person
Yeah, um hum! Dat's right!
Yeah
wonda if dey 'no' dey do dat to us?
I bet dey don' EB'N 'no' -

Lemme as' ya'll som'n' else.
Y'all eba notice dat
some white folk still don' believ'
dat Black folk 'no' how da think,
analyze, or reason, too.
Yeah, um hum! Dat's right!
Wonda if dey 'no' dey do dat to us?
I bet dey don' EB'N 'no".
Lemme as' y'all som'n' else.
Y'all eba notice dat
some white folk still don' understan'
dat when ya work hard
and ya ain't on welfare
ya can buy what ya wanna buy -
wit yo' OWN money.
Yeah, um hum! Dat's right!
Wonda if dey 'no' dey do dat ta us?
I bet dey don' EB'N 'no'.

Lemme as' y'all one mo' then
Y'all eba notice dat some white folks think
dey got all…………da brains?
Think dey got 'em ALL!
Yeah, uh hum! Dat's right!
Wonda if dey 'no' dey do dat to us?
I bet dey don' EB'N 'no'.

Now dis da las' thin'
sho' nuf now.
Y'all eba notice dat
SOME BLACK FOLK jus' is bad,
'bout some of dis stuff is white folks?
Yeah, um hum! Dat's right!
Wonda if dey 'no' dey "crazy," too?
I bet dey don' EB'N 'no'.

Bettye Stevens Coney

A BLACK CHILD'S PLEA
(Please Help Me)

I want to learn. I want to know.
I want to grow up so I can be like Mr. and Mrs.
Folks, you know.

I want to be somebody. I have to beat the odds,
because if I don't I'll end up in a world
of uncaring nods.

Please, help me! I need you now!
My daddy's gone and I don't know where.
But sometimes he calls just to see if we're there.

Please, help me! I need you now!
I want to make something of myself - but don't know how.
In spite of my weaknesses, In spite of my line -
I silently cry for a better world for my sister,
brother and all mankind.

Please, help me! You, there, who
know so much more than I.

Give me a chance. Lend me an ear.
Don't give up on me yet.
If you give up on me, no one else will care.

My Soul Speaks Truth

TELL THEM

Tell the Media and tell the shows:
All Black youth don't fight and strike blows!
Some are about staying in school,
studying hard, following the rules.

Tell the writer to cast the plays
Show Black youth in positives ways,
taking home books, making good grades,
graduating school, all subjects made.

Tell the editor and tell the press:
Write of us in a way to express
All Black youth aren't corrupt and mad.
Usually, they slant us to look bad.

Tell the manager in public stores:
We don't all steal while walking the floors!
our reputation, we must guard -
for ourselves and parents who work hard.

Tell the policeman and tell the chief:
Every Black child is not a thief!
Stereo-typical thinking must cease.
See us as human beings not beasts.

Tell the school teacher in the classroom:
All Blacks aren't dull, headed for doom.
Give us a chance, the lesson to learn;
Show us you care and you're concerned.

Tell the whole world, in waiting out there:
Black youth of America everywhere
deserve to be seen with eyes "untaunted".
Tell some good things; it's all warranted!

TELL THEM!

Bettye Stevens Coney

SAD

It's a sad day
in the USA
No more parental controlling
of (a generation of) children's
upbringing and traditional molding.

Sad
When a parent's fear of HRS
prevents them from applying their rules
and children putting their parents to the test,
screaming:
"I'll call 911",
slams the door
then starts to run.

Sad
How we're losing great minds.
some of our children are going astray
because our family structure has declined.
Now you and I know
we'll not throw our hands up
in utter dismay
until we have found a way
to rescue our future
and save the day.

WAKE UP, AMERICA, WAKE UP!

The ruthless killings must stop
Black, White and other people of color, too,
killing the young and the old.
They prove they have no consciousness, no soul.

Wake up, America, wake up.
We must face the problem head on
let folks know up front:
"When you kill, for no reason at all,
there's no need to stall
You kill! You die! You fry!"

Unsafe are our homes and our streets.
Unsafe are our cars and our parks.
Unsafe are the public places we meet.

How long must we continue to be
prisoners in America, the land of the free.
We must protect the innocent people.
Please, America, act now!

Bettye Stevens Coney

TAKING APPLICATIONS
(To Join Club Rainbow Race)

Yes. You may step right up, please.
I'll put your worries at ease.
No. You won't have to compete.
Come right in and have a seat.

Here's your application, Sir.
Fill all spaces, I'd prefer.
Thank you for coming today.
Now, I'll explain if I may.

You have taken a giant step.
Yes. The whole world you can help.
By Joining Club Rainbow Race,
Mankind you'll meet face to face.

At the table we shall sit
to talk. Nothing we'll omit.
Black, White, Red, Brown and Yellow -
We'll respect each kind fellow.

We will make a petition,
Solving conflicts - our mission.
In each village and each town,
Spread applications all around.

A better world, we shall make,
If seriously you take
This message from me to you,
Then greater things we'll pursue

Join up today, everyone.
I bet we can have great fun,
Seeing that each has a heart,
Willing to share - peace to impart.

GENUINE KINDNESS KNOWS NO RACE

Genuine Kindness Knows No Race
Are you your brother's keeper
regardless of face?
I've met many people
on this journey in life
who shared from their heart,
speaking kind words, treating me awfully nice
There are so many of these
precious moments in time
I've experienced this oneness -
harmony, peace
and sameness in mind

The other day, in a parking lot
an elderly lady
became misplaced from her car
I noticed her
being hot, fatigued, confused
coming back in the store
So I opened the door
She noticeably needed help
I asked what's the matter?
Said she needed to find her car
I knew
it couldn't have been far
I assisted her with packages
found her a seat in the cool
I was willing to help,
didn't have any thing to lose
With a gentleman's help
we roamed the parking lot
looking for the description
of what might be her car
In a distance
we spotted afar
her white, Nebraska tag, Ford Taurus
station wagon car
I drove it in front of the store
while the gentleman

Bettye Stevens Coney

Genuine Kindness Knows No Race, Page 2

> escorted her through the door
> To the car she then proceeded
> but before she entered in
> guess what happened then?
> She hugged and kissed me
> so thankfully
> Her lips knew no color then
> and I cared not about a face
> For helping someone in need
> is not a matter of race.

LEVEL V

COME FLY WITH ME

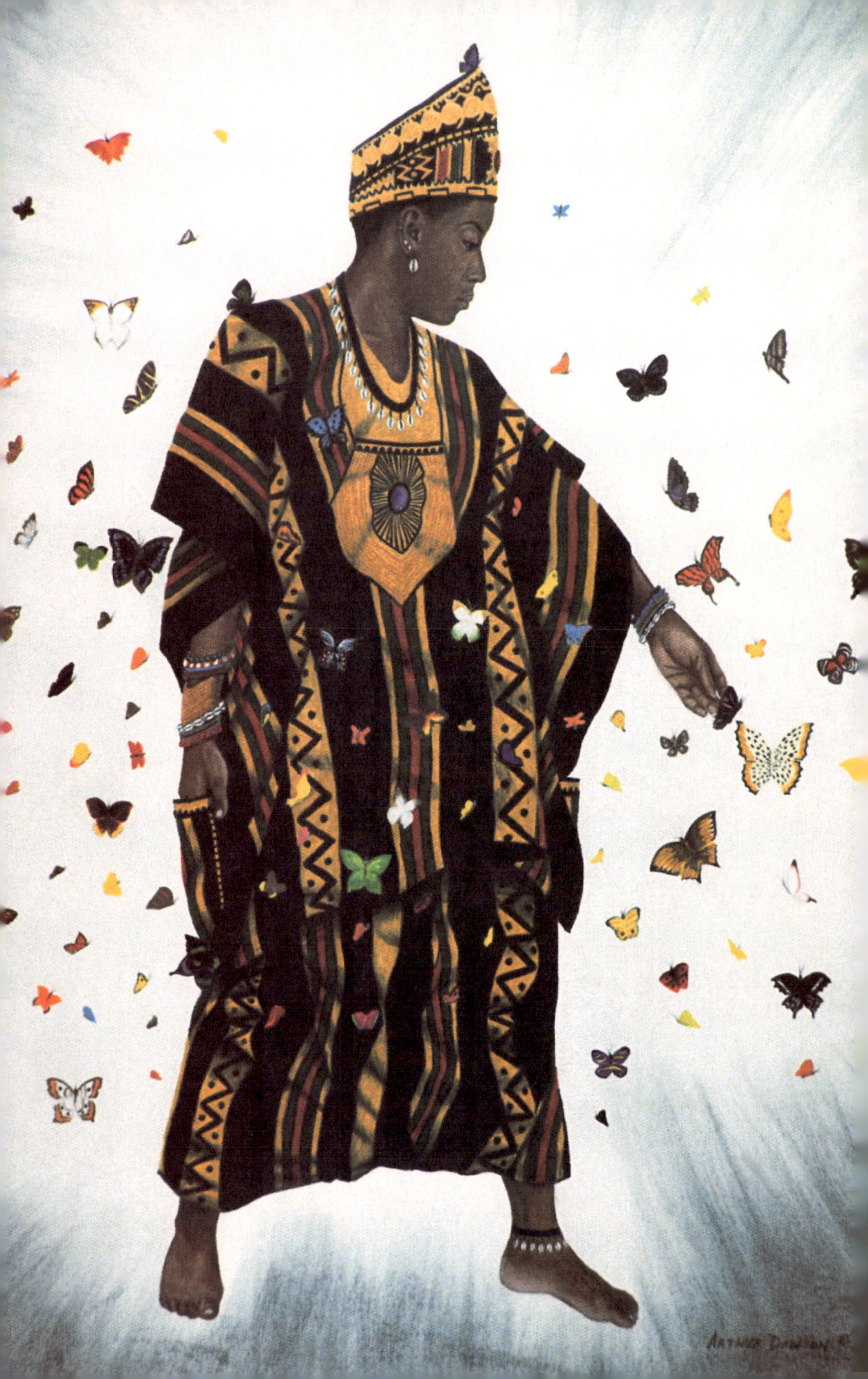

COME FLY WITH ME

When my mind is in flight with hope, it transcends me to, beautiful places, where possibilities are limitless, where negative experiences have no significance and where the future is bright and promising for everyone who desires it to be SO.

In this positive state of mind (which is where I live most of the time), I believe that I have been blessed with the special gift of motivating, stimulating, and inspiring the satisfied and unconcerned among us. I have a stirring passion to lift up the downtrodden and unmotivated who are headed nowhere as well as the able, talented people.

Whether male or female, young or old, Black, White, Brown, Yellow or Red, people must be given a vision or a ray of hope for life.

More than anything, I long for the appropriate words to articulate the urgency of the hour to our young people who take so much of life for granted.

Together, we can help change our world.

Let us all Come Fly Together.

Bettye Stevens Coney

SHARING TO BE FREE

The mind within
Is mighty strong indeed -
Impulses no longer to wait
Nor thoughts that I care to impede.

Emotions - stored on the shelf of time -
Talents, gifts and experiences
Anxiously pausing in line.

Now I know why, for years, I've cringed, cried
And sighed -
Simply because, I realize now, there's more,
Much more of me inside.

Though numerous times I've wondered
What else He's ordained for me -
Now, believing the time has come
I see - it is more of my inner self
I must Share - to be free.

Whether it's a song to sing
A poem to pin
or a heart to cheer, and try to win

of all these things
That are part of me
I must share them totally - totally
...to be free.

BUT, WHY CAN'T I

But, why can't I?
"Just do as you're told to do.
Don't ask, 'Why'?
Ask me no questions,
And I'll tell you no lie."

But, why can't I
rise to the height
of my intelligence, too?
Bet I can fly
Just as high as you.

But, why can't I
trust you
to look at me
as your equal, too?

Don't you see?
Two minds are better than one.
Let's soar together
Until the victory's won.

Bettye Stevens Coney

MIND OVER FEAR

Let me tell you something, Folks
This important thing I speak.
Just in case you haven't realized
Fear, like deadly venom, makes everybody weak.

Take heed to this, My People
Fear comes from negative thoughts
Placed in your mind by the devil.
Don't be so cheaply bought.

Listen to me, My People -
Fear plays tricks on your mind,
Saying you can't do this or that.
Never concede to that tormenting line.

Fear damns you, and dogs you.
Fear deems you unfit.
Fear chases you like a mad man
Down in some bottomless pit.

You were born for a purpose;
You are destined to win.
Put your mind over matter,
Set your sights and begin

I will be your role model;
It's my mission, I believe.
But listen to me very carefully
This lesson you must receive.

No one else can pull you up
From amidst those rocks and stones.
Take charge of your destiny.
It's yours to do alone.

Mind over Fear, Page 2

Positive thoughts produce positive actions
They highlight your very best.
It's the process necessary for your unfolding.
Refuse to accept anything less.

Mind over fear, it's up to you.
Allow yourself to dream.
Let your imagination rise to its height
Things are not always what they seem.

What happens next can be the awakening
of a new person, a brand new you,
Rising to do the impossible
And showing forth that which is true.

Learn to enjoy your new self.
See the beginning of each new day
As an opportunity to be successful
By functioning in an affirmative way.

Stand tall. Think big.
And above all, stay strong.
Advance to pick up another -
Someone who's headed wrong.

Bettye Stevens Coney

SELF-MOTIVATION

Self-motivation is the key -
It's a necessary ingredient for you and me.
It enhances success in life;
It keeps you going,
When no one tells you,
"Good job, very nice."

Self-motivation makes you get up and go:
It won't let you sit around and throw
Away your precious talents anymore.

Self-motivation tells you you're somebody special:
It stimulates your inner being;
It provides vision worth seeing.

Self-motivation keeps you going strong:
It gives you renewed strength and vitality;
And molds your dreams into reality.

Self-motivation enables you to come alive:
It brings your innermost treasures outside
And causes success to abide.

EVER WONDER HOW IT HAPPENS TO BE

Ever wonder how it happens to be,
When at the close of day
You feel uplifted and fulfilled
Because you were so impressed
To share of your earthly goods
And simply give.

Ever wonder how it happens to be,
When at the close of day,
You go inside yourself to search and see
And find enclosed in a sacred place,
All the ingredients for the making of one
Who must be mentally and spiritually free.

Ever wonder how it happens to be,
When at the close of day,
You ponder in gray areas and find
Your style of living is all predicated on
A positive state of mind.

Bettye Stevens Coney

THE NEUTRAL RACE

The neutral race
is a beautiful race.
It's the race I like to see.
It's made of the peoples of the world,
people like you and me.

The neutral race
is just a face.
and only sees the mind.
It is the race that has no color
and treats everybody kind.

The neutral race
is a smiling face
that sees only with the heart.
It judges every man on how he stands
and peace and love imparts.

COME ON, SISTER GIRL!

Your speeches I hear;
Your songs I enjoy -
I observe your ways
And the lessons you employ.

Your words are profound,
No lies can be traced.
You're a woman of this age -
Come take your rightful place.

You rap to your children -
Of both truth and deceit -
Your words of wisdom,
Save from defeat.

Come on, Sister Girl!
Muster up your ambitions,
Stir up your initiative,
Show your intentions.
Come on, Sister Girl!
Take charge once more.
Together, we can go far -
Let's open the door.

Come on, Sister Girl!
You can make it, if you dare.
Just don't give up.
There's a wonderful world out there.

Keep your focus centered
And your motivation high.
Continue to climb
Until you reach the sky.

Come on, Sister Girl!
I see you everyday,
Sitting in silence
With nothing to say.
Come on, Sister Girl!
Success is yours for the asking.
Put yourself in gear
And prepare for action!

Sister Girl! this advice I give:
Wisdom is the teacher of time,
But let faith be
The anchor for your mind.

LEVEL VI

LOVING

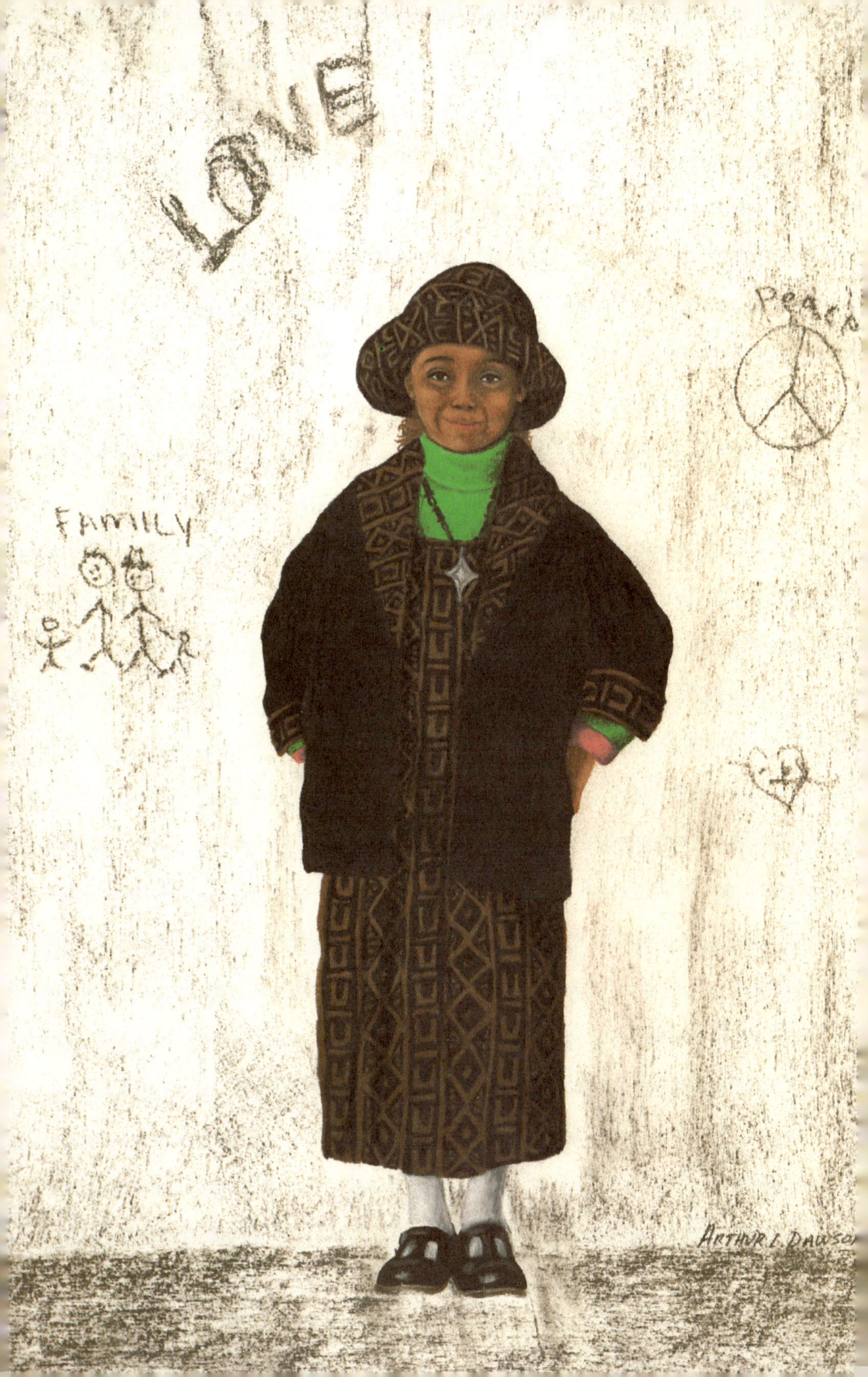

LOVING

My experience with love is described this way - a fullness in the depth of my inner being, passionately dripping, crisp, fresh vapors, foaming tons of atoms in the crust and crevices of my soul.

That continuous flow, igniting from its rich source of fresh vapor, makes it possible for me to go on from day to day. It's me. It's what I am about.

Whether it is in interacting with my God, my parents when they lived, the man in my life, my daughters and family, children or my friends, it's that wholeness and quality of my self that I share. My love knows few boundaries. It's pure. It's eternal.

Bettye Stevens Coney

FAMILY

Family
is one of
the most beautiful words
in the world to me.
With only six letters,
I declare its melody.

Family means
ancestry and inheritance so swell.
The family history presents to us
a record of people, places and things as well.
We dig far back into our roots
and we may find golden, hidden treasures –
all tucked away in old books,
bringing to us delight and pleasures.
Then we turn back the hands of time
and, like a wide, vivid cinemax screen,
we see our lineage so fine.
Though we see
a path of struggle, pain and toil,
also, we see
how love and faith sustained us all,
and we see
men, women, boys and girls there -
All our people,
whose genes we now proudly share
and in a distance we can see
our offspring in years to come,
researching the past as we've done
to see where they have come from.

Family means
sharing with others.
It's giving and taking, too.
It's love both tried and true.

Family, Page 2

Family means
who and what you are -
It's all that you're about.
It's meaningful relationships, not clout.

Family means
in-laws, precious and kind.
It's making two families as one.
It's loving, caring and fun.

Family means
freedom and peace.
It's our secured playing field,
our protection and our shield.

Bettye Stevens Coney

TALKING WITH UNCLE ESSIE

That Sunday morning, after church
at Sykes Savannah
United Methodist Church
in Bells, South Carolina,
I asked Uncle Essie
to ride with me
because I wanted to see
how much about my roots
he could tell me.
At age ninety-six,
though hard of hearing,
his memory was still in tact.
Soon I learned
likewise
were the facts.

Growing up,
I'd often heard it said,
"Your great-granddaddy Dan'l
looked white."
"Sister", Papa Dudy
and all the rest
same words they could attest.
How it came to be,
I didn't know specifics, but it interested me.

It was common knowledge
among all the old folks.
I'd heard it said time and time again
That's how you get
your golden red skin.
Just wanted to know more
so our history
I would show
in a family reunion of the century.
I called near and far
"Let's bring ourselves together
to see who we are."
While on the way
to Uncle Essie's house
my mouth stood open
as he had his say.

Talking with Uncle Essie, Page 2

> I was amazed.
> I was thrilled.
> I drove along in a mystical daze,
> so impressed was I.
> He still remembered;
> He spoke without a sigh.
>
> Then quickly I thought,
> Uncle Essie,
> a tape recorder I've brought.
> Wait 'til we get to your house
> our history you can announce.
> Soon to his place, we arrived.
> From the car, we departed;
> into the house, we entered.
> Other family members were there -
> all of us
> joyfully assembled
>
> Into the living room, we settled.
> Uncle Essie and I
> sat in a corner far away
> from the others –
> I thought.
> So I took out
> the recorder I'd brought
>
> Taping Time!
>
> Now, Uncle Essie, I said,
> speaking in an elevated voice.
> Because of the chattering crowd,
> I had to speak loud(ly).
> Please, start from the beginning.
> Tell me the Stephens' Story.
> "Eh-----," he said,
> posturing forward his tall,
> handsome frame.
> Tell me the Stephens' Story again;
> tell me from beginning to end
>
> "But I don' tol' ya, one time."
> Speaking in his slow, soft, loving voice,
> he couldn't quite figure out
> Why repeat?
> Was I in doubt?

Bettye Stevens Coney

Talking with Uncle Essie, Page 3

Uncle Essie, I said.
Please, tell me again.
"What you say?"

"Eh --------
"Say you gon' call?"
Yes, Sir, I want to RECORD IT.

He began ----
"Rubin Stephens
was de ole slave master".

"Dat's where Stephens Cross Road
come from."
"Ain't I don' tol' you dat?
I don' tol' ya dat one time."

TAKE ONE
INSTRUCTION TIME

Uncle Essie, I said.
Please don't say
you don' tol' me dat.
Remember, we're taping.
This is history
you're making.

"Eh -------------------"
Don't answer back that way.
Tell the story straight
if you may.
"Okay.
Hee, hee, hee," he laughed.

Our session
we started again.
Just gotta get our history
from way back then.

"Rubin had a son," he said.
"His name was Levi.
Levi had a son from a beautiful
Black slave girl.
Her name was Judy.
Dan'l was Levi and Judy's son;
Levi was the ole slave master's son.
You understand?

Talking with Uncle Essie, Page 4

Dan'l was my daddy
De ole slave master's son, Levi
was my granddaddy."

"Dey tell me dat
Levi wanted to keep Dan'l,
and did keep him
for a little while."
Those words he spoke
with a smile.
"But didn't keep 'em long
CAUSE Judy didn't let 'em."
He continued.
"Dan'l had seventeen children,"
he said.
They were from
two women he'd wed.

Do you remember
all of their names?
"Yeah,
Ain' I don' tol' ya dat, too?"

Yes, Sir.

"Why ya ast me agin?"

Please, Sir.
Tell me once more.
I began to wonder then
if I were a bore!

"Dudy was de oldest.
Dat was ya gran'daddy."
Yes, Sir, I remember him.
"Yeah."
"Den dere was Alice Cornelia,
Essie, dat's me."
That's right.
You're the oldest living now
"Yeah. I'm ninety-six years old.
Hee, hee, hee."
He laughed
with gusto and glee.

He continued naming Dan'l's children:
"Calip was next,
Wilfred, Milton, Mary Ann Melissa,

Bettye Stevens Coney

Talking with Uncle Essie, Page 5

    Walter, Angus, Leavy,
    Ella, Lucius, Bud,
    Julia, Herb, and Harvey
    was de baby."

    He gave to me
    that day
    history unequaled
    to pay.

    In July of 1977,
    with the help of many,
    I had a dream come true.
    I did what I believed
    was ordained me to do -
    that was
    bring together
    The Stephens Crew.

    We worshipped God;
    We celebrated our roots;
    We made a roll call,
    naming grandparents,
    seeing descendants and all.

    Little less than five hundred
    were fed that day -
    They came from near and far.
    They came by chartered bus,
    airplane, train and car,
    all coming to get an account
    of who we are.

    Talking with Uncle Essie
    will always be
    etched in the memories of my mind
    as one of
    the most precious
    moments in time.

VISITING UP HOME

How're you, Cous'n Lizabeth?
"Ain't nut'n mu's te me, Mazie.
Got dis ole a'sridus en me knee
Ketch me so bad som'tim'.
Kin hardly go."
Oh?
I'm so sorry to hear that, Cous'n Lizabeth.
"But I keeps go'in.
By da hep of de Lo'd.
Thank God, it ain't no badder den it tis, chil'."
Yes, M'am.

"Lo'd, I sho' is glad da see ye'na"
It's always a pleasure to see you,
Cous'n Lizabeth.

"Phalmus, ye'na ain' ga have no mo' chillin?"
Don' seem like it, Cous'n Lizabeth.

"She ga be tall like you, Phalmus.
Look gis like you spit der out che mout'.
Got dat pudy smile like you, Mazie.
Wha' sho name is?"
My name is Bettye.
"Humm."

"Ye'na still live dow ney 'n Flada, a?"
Yes m'am. We're still there.

"Now whey's ya brothers, Son 'in' Eddie at?"
Son's in Charleston.
And Eddie's in Jacksonville.
"Humm."

"I sho's glad da see ye'na.
Coase ye'na always did come 'n' see 'bout me.
Hee, hee."

I'm ready to go now, Daddy.
"Dese chillin ka'n be still long, kin dey?
Whey ya gwin go, chile?"
I'm just ready to go, Cousin Lizabeth.

Bettye Stevens Coney

Visiting Up Home, Page 2

"Wait, chere.
Guin git ya som' dese 'madas I canned."
Let's go Daddy.

Oh, thanks so much, Cous'n Lizabeth.
You take this and buy youself something.

"Ooh, me Lo'd,
I sho thank ya.
God guin bless ye'na fa dis.
Hee, hee.
Thank ye'na."

We'd better be going now, Cous'n Lizabeth.
"Ye'na com' back ag'in,
Ya yeah."
Bye, Cous'n Elizabeth.

BEAUTIFUL PEOPLE

Both Mama and Daddy
were beautiful people -
one short, one tall,
but infinitely equal.
Mama was dark
and Daddy was light.
Together they made me
and I'm just right.

Mama was an angel
with a beautiful smile.
She had high cheek bones,
much like Indian style.
The radiance of Mama's presence
set the whole world aglow.
Her speech sounded rehearsed,
but is wasn't a show.

To me Daddy was the handsomest
of all the men I'd seen -
always kind and polite,
never ugly or mean.
My Daddy was generous
for beyond measure.
He never asked for repay;
He said it was his pleasure.

Mama was brilliant,
used to teach school -
readin', 'ritin', 'rithmetic,
and the golden rule.
A special thrill I receive
when I hear people say,
"Your Mama was so sweet,
and you are just that way."

Mama and Daddy -
In the choir, I watched them sing.
Their voices blended together
in a sacred, harmonious ring.
Then by and by,
Graduation Day came.
Both now live with God
on His celestial plane.

Bettye Stevens Coney

MY BABY GIRL

She's as precious as can be;
So endearing is she to me.
My baby girl.
The perfect baby if ever there was
Thank God for his blessing of love.

From cuddling and cooing, too
And putting on a mix matched shoe.
My baby girl.
What joy she brings to my heart;
To this family a most important part.

Each realm of growth and development
Brings new dimensions of excitement.
My baby girl.
She's God's little creation sent from above -
Pretty, smart and full of his love.

In awe I sit and stare -
Perfect her face and hair.
My baby girl.
With her daddy's eyes and nose,
Tall and looks like me, I suppose.

Her personality is all her own -
She's independent to the bone.
My baby girl.
She's made me mighty proud,
Standing far above the crowd.

In the corporate world,
She's created a swirl.
No more my baby girl
She's a fine young woman now.
I thank you, God,....and how!

WHEN SHE WAS BORN

When she was born,
I sensed there was
total agreement,
agreement between the earth,
the sky, My Maker and me.
When at first
I conceived -
two lovers, fulfilling a dream
to form another life
by the oneness of our bodies,
nestled in rapture so nice.
Then, that awesome moment occurred -
His profound joy,
united with my
divine hope,
created a majestic symphony.
All our own
playing, melodically, rhythmically -
together we composed a score of music,
a musical script
that brought to us
a rhapsody of love and fulfillment
for our entire lives.
Her name is
Melodi.

Bettye Stevens Coney

SHE'S DADDY'S DELIGHT

Can't you see?
She's Daddy's Delight -
Says he won't do this or that,
Bet he will with all his might

Daddy's bark
Is bigger than his bite.
She knows how
To please his appetite

She says, "Daddy"
In tones just right
And to her music he plays
without a fight.

She and her daddy,
They're very much alike:

He, his piece of paper
With notes to do today,
Everybody just knows
That's his way.

And everyday at work or play
She has her planner
Doing as Daddy does
in like manner.

Daddy just knows
His girl is smart and bright
She's his Melodi -
She's Daddy's Delight.

TO HER LOVELINESS

My Mama
was a beautiful, brown woman,
very stately
though not very tall.
When you'd see her,
you just knew
she was intelligent,
proud,
well raised and all.
Of course
she would never
call
any attention to herself.
She was just
"Mazie"
that's all,
sweet, kind,
and amazing.
She walked with an air
of sheer grace,
self assured, but not "uppity"
(or with pretense).
Softly-and calmly, she'd explain herself
never was there any quarreling.
She was
everybody's darling.
Her character was humble and kind,
peaceful and sublime.
It was a family tradition,
a legacy
left behind.
Now,
I'm challenged
to emulate her -
a charge
that's hard indeed.
What I sense
she's saying to me this day
in her quiet,
serene way:
"My Child,
you too
can be like Mama
Just stay
on bended knees
and pray."

Bettye Stevens Coney

HEY! LITTLE RED HEAD GIRL

Here she come,
walkin' down dat road ag'in.
Hey! Little Red Head Girl,
wit' yo' hair
the same color as yo' skin.
Dat sun's mighty hot
out dere ya in,
Hey! Little Red Head Girl,
how many times
ya been to the sto' today?
Wearin' dat pretty li'l dress
wit' pleats and ruffles,
neatly pressed.
How much fo' dat strawberry soda
did ya pay?
Little Red Head Girl,
go to da sto' ev'ryday!
She go' to the Barrett sto'
not fa away.
Dey kno' what she want
soon as she walk in the do'.
Den home she go
to lay on the front porch flo',
sippin' red soda
once mo'.

ONLY CHILDREN
(An only Child)

Only children are
one of a kind.
They're independent
and creative in mind.
They're not selfish in the least -
just need to be shown
love, harmony and peace.
Only children are your comrades,
indeed.
They'll always be there,
your friend
when you're in need.
Only children can be
in their world
all alone
and see beautiful people
without hatred or scorn.
They've a sense of true love.
When hearts infinitely beat,
they give to you
their emotions to keep.
only children long for
companionship so dear.
They long to be
loved, cuddled
by you,
with you.
Always near.

THERE'S A LITTLE CHURCH I KNOW
(New Bethel A. M. E., Okahumpka, Florida)

There's a little church I know.-
It hardly seems to grow.
I was reared in that church
and I love it very much.

Mama and Daddy sat first pew;
Everybody there they knew.
That Sunday I was christened,
all were there, nobody missin'.

In that little church of mine,
families were mighty fine.
Everybody was mostly kin
or had same place origin.

We'd all go to Sunday School -
practiced the golden rule.
Then morning service we'd go,
all dressed from head to toe.

Many of us at that time,
were children in our prime.
Together we'd mostly sit;
sometimes gave our parents a fit.

We'd pass notes and sniggle
about ladies' struts and wiggles;
and always we'd find
mischief for our minds.

There's A Little Church I Know, cont.

When "determinations" were told,
members spoke very bold
about their journey to heaven
and broke the bread of leaven.

Then our time came to speak,
we spoke soft and meek;
said we'd go to heaven, too.
That's all we ever knew.

In unison our speech we mastered.
Gave our hand to the Pastor;
Said, "We're members now;
Gotta be good anyhow."

We all grew up day by day;
Each learning along the way.
Then high school graduation came
But the past remains the same.

Those who grew up in that church
were blessed very much
by the teachings of the old -
"To God's hand forever hold."

And now all of us are grown,
have children of our own.
Still loving memories are there -
forget them not, I dare.

Bettye Stevens Coney

MY MAN AND HIS SAX

He's tall, medium brown, handsome
and not too thin.
When he plays his sax
it's everybody's
attention
he wins.
With fingers in position
and eyes closed just so;
hear him play
.and you'll know he's a musician -
and excellent show.
From his soul,
he plays
and to the audience
he serenades.
He can make that "axe"
SING
ANYTHING!

He makes that sax of his sound
as though
there are micro tiny
human voices
being piped through the column
of the instrument
producing
most musical forms
from bellowing blues
and
lamenting spirituals
to the sacred church songs
and upbeat gospels
to
ragtime, swing
and classy, sassy jazz
to
Mozart, Bach, Rimsky-Korsakof,
Tschaikowsky, Debussy, Gershwin
and all those men.

My Man and His Sax
are hard to beat.
Just listen to him play
and you, too, will say,
"He's GREAT!
Let's book him for a date."

FROM THE PRINCIPAL
(RIMES ELEMENTARY SCHOOL)

I have observed how hard you work with
students and how much you care.
I have observed how diligently you plan
and prepare.
I have observed how your face lights up
with glee, when students remember and
answer questions book free.
I have observed your depression near,
how when your students misbehave and
you must interfere.
I have observed how proud you are,
when in single line your students form,
whether going to the cafeteria, music,
media or PE platform.
I have observed you. I have observed you.
And though your pay may not reflect
your worth, and valuable time spent may
not appear to scratch the surf,
our boys and girls love you, that's for
sure or haven't you noticed through the
thick and thin, the subject matter they'll
master and endure, to the end.
And I. I who am the leader of the flock,
I who dream of a better world for boys and
girls on the block -
I shall always remember you in my
special prayer, because you show our
students that you really care.

Bettye Stevens Coney

TRUE FRIENDS ARE

Irreplaceable,, immovable, untouchable
and irresistible....
are true friends.
They're
lovable, huggable, adorable,
admirable and gullible....
They're
caring, sharing, giving, providing,
letting and lending.
When we're together we act:
sane, silly, intelligent, crazy,
sincere and sensible.
When one needs the other, we:
stop, go, attend, serve, act,
do and mend.
When we see each other, we:
greet, meet, laugh, talk,
whine and dine.
When we don't see each other, we:
call, write, inquire, search,
seek and find.
When one feels down or depressed,
we: listen, question, reason, motivate,
suggest or solve.
When one feels defeated, we:
uplift, inspire, excite,
stimulate and encourage.
When one achieves, we:
congratulate, recognize, honor, applaud,
celebrate and congregate.

That's what True Friends Are.

I REMEMBER THE DAYS

I remember the days when all of us were there
I remember the days when none were in despair.

I remember the days when laughter
was light and gay; and activities -
though short, simple and sincere,
were all part of the families that were near.

I remember the days, oh, how sweet and so dear.
They have come and gone yet
the memories linger forever and a year.

I remember the days when
the Thanksgiving meal I first prepared;
how eager, excited and the feeling -
It was my premier!
For me it was a great endeavor,
but I didn't flutter a feather.
For I was grateful to everyone
for their recipes they shared.

I remember the Thanksgiving meal ….
so much food, so tasty, I thought:
it's my cooking, how unreal!

I remember the days when all of us were there;
I remember the days when none were in despair.

I remember the days when
Mama and Daddy were there;
they, so proud and I so thankful.

So thankful to God for blessing me
with parents who unconditionally
shared their love with me.

I remember the days when all of us were there;
now they've gone to that great, sweet somewhere.

I LOVE LAUGHING

I love laughing.
I love making other people laugh.
I love being with people who make me laugh.

When I laugh, all of me is happy
When I'm happy, all of me is well.
When I laugh, I feel wonderful inside.
When I laugh, nothing comes out sounding
    poised and refined.
When I laugh, I feel joy way down in my toes.
When I laugh, I don't care who hears or knows.

I love laughing. I've never tried to resist.
Laughing energizes, magnetizes and entices cheer.

I just love laughing - it's like medicine they say.
I just love laughing - everyone seems to be in love
    that way.

I love laughing. Laugh along with me and
    feel the joy it brings.
Laugh along with me; inspire your spirit
    with a laugh.

Laugh away your cares.
Laugh away your fears.
You'll feel better when you
    learn to laugh.

Try out your laughing box -
See how deep and strong it is inside.
Bet you haven't had a good laugh in years.
Got too much pride?

Better get rid of that burden.
Come on and laugh with me, World.
Stop that hurting.

LEVEL VII

THE HOLY SPIRIT WITHIN

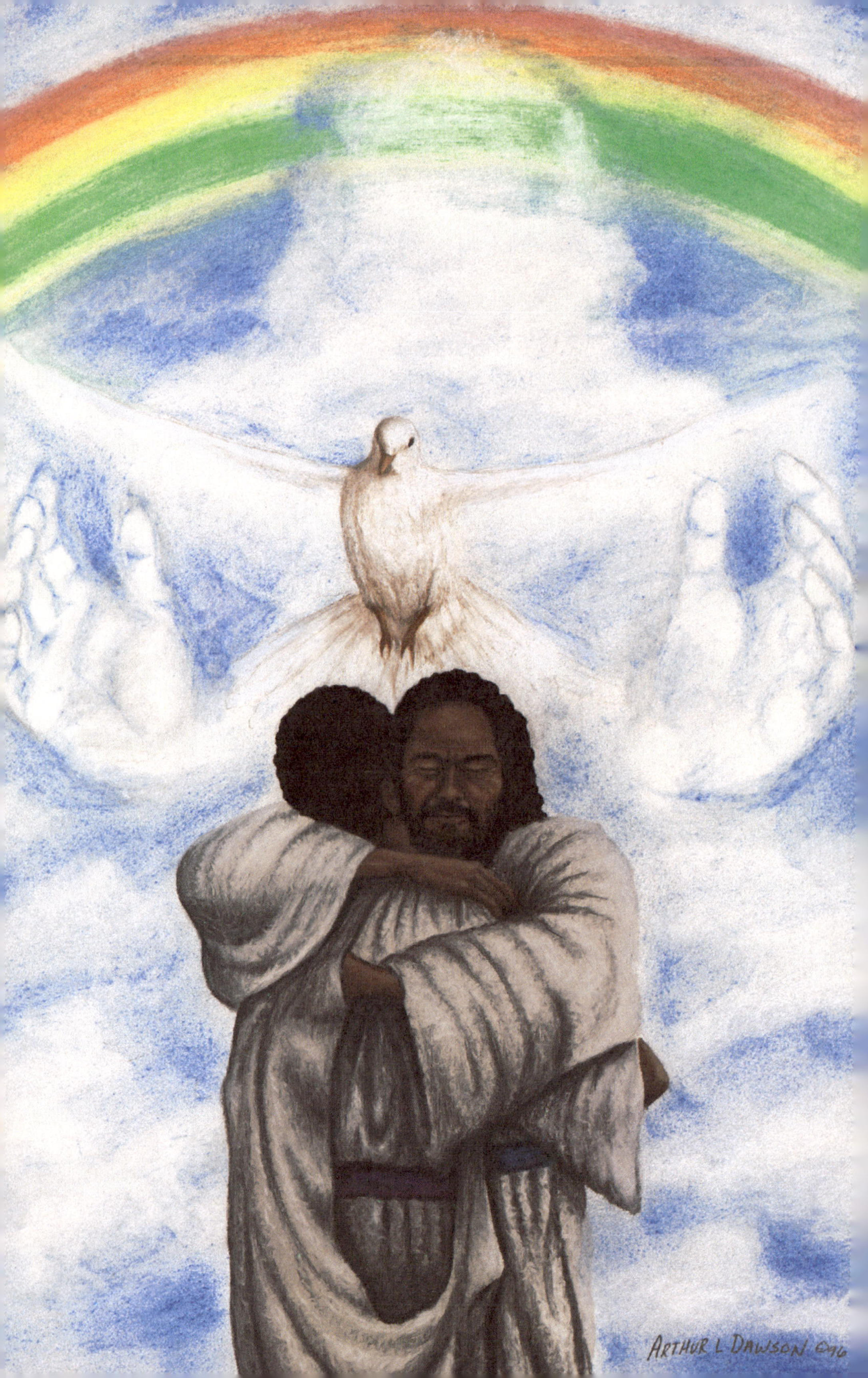
ARTHUR L DAWSON ©96

THE HOLY SPIRIT WITHIN

I believe the Supreme Being in my life communicates with me according to my individual uniqueness.

That being in my life is Jesus.

I confess his Lordship in my life, and I make no apologies.

Remember when we first met, I told you about my upbringing? I mentioned to you that my parents were humble, God-fearing people. Consequently, they taught their daughter to be of the same faith.

As I began to mature, I began to search for TRUTH for myself. I just had to have a personal experience with whoever or whatever it was that was responsible for my eternal being. I had to know more about this ALMIGHTY, ALL SEEING, ALL KNOWING, OMNIPOTENT SOURCE to which Mama and Daddy referred. But, not only that, I developed an insatiable desire to find out if there was more to this Supreme Being than the gruesome "hell fire and damnation" part that many preachers preached about on Sunday mornings.

The path of my search and inquisitiveness led me (by way of an horrifying experience with the Ouija board and a seance) to realize that the Christian guidance Mama and Daddy gave me was all that I needed all along. As I sought a closer relationship with the Supreme Being in my life, He became my personal friend. I know Him and I know He knows my name is Bettye Jean Stevens Coney.

So, I have learned to talk with Him, The Holy Spirit Within, as though He were another person. Not only do I confer with Him about moving mountains in my way, but I consult Him for little things too - finding a parking space or helping me locate pretty shoes for my size 10 narrow feet or assisting me in finding important misplaced items. I have also prayed The Speeders Prayer: "O, Lord, please don't let it be me that flashing light is coming for..." Now Y'all know y'all done prayed dat one too...

The Jesus that I have come to know in my life is a marvelous experience. He's my ever abundant, ever present source. Although with my persistent, right now nature, He sometimes does not respond as immediately as I would like Him, but as the saying goes, "He's always right on time."

Bettye Stevens Coney

The greatest fulfillment in my life is knowing there is an Almighty Source to whom I can go and with whom I can have a very personal relationship. He's miraculous. He's TRULY AWESOME! No. I am by no means perfect - still got some quirks to work out. But I long for His presence with me and I seek his guidance daily.

I am so wonderfully blessed to have this kind of friend — THE HOLY SPIRIT WITHIN.

MY SUPERNATURAL FRIEND
(The Holy Spirit)

While talking to true friends,
there's no need to worry
when
you'll hear your words again.
Like the feeling on the skin of cool salve,
friends are a comfort to have.
But
I MUST tell you about my truest friend:
He's ALWAYS there -
ALWAYS on His post -
to answer me whenever I need Him most.
He and I
make such a perfect pair.
He brings me peace
when I'm in despair.
He provides me calm
when others may not care.
When in conflict,
and my mind raves and wrestles,
I go to Him.
He leads me to His Epistles.
There
I can see clearly
His answer to my query.
When in secret
I feel rejected,
I go to Him
and He reassures me that I,
I am His own
and I am never alone.
When
sometimes life may seem unkind
and the way seems dark and dreary,

Bettye Stevens Coney

My Supernatural Friend, Page 2

       He says to me:
       "Be not afraid and be not weary.
       I have your back.
       My Promises are fact.
       I am your God!
       Lean on me and I will make your burdens
       light and your way easy.
       Remember
       It is I who provide the wind
       for the sparrow to fly and the eagle to soar.
       Don't you know?
       It is for you that I want much more."
       Yes.
       When I go to Him
       in manner sincere,

       I always come away feeling refreshed
       and in high gear.

       He's My Super Natural Friend –
       The Holy Spirit within.

AWESOME, POWERFULLY AWESOME

Many times I'd read those verses,
given to me over two decades ago.
I didn't understand exactly what He
was saying to me,
nor where He was pointing me to go.

Each time I read the Chapter,
I just knew there were special jewels
contained therein for me.
only the time had not come for me to see how
and when the mystery would be.

Although something inside my spirit
quickly identified itself with that printed page
and called it mine for sure (I know),
there was my name posted all over that Scripture,
and none else did see, but me.

Again and Again I read it....
eagerly wondering and longing for the day
when I would be brought face to face
with His timing, seeing and discovering
more of His Amazing Grace.

My, how long it has taken for me
to grow, mature, develop and ripen,
just so I would have the words to show
that He moves in His time.
And at that time, I shall know.

Each day now, the meaning of the verses
move closer to my understanding
and closer to the reality of what
He meant then and begins to evolve, now,
in my life today.

His blessings, talents and gifts
I must now share for others to see
and be equally, blissfully blessed.
Awesome, Powerfully Awesome, He Is to Me!

Bettye Stevens Coney

HE SHOWS ME HE'S THERE

A friend and I met,
a time we had set.
Just to talk and pray,
seeking what He'd say.

She said to me how
His Spirit allows
her to know he's there
when sometimes in prayer.

Amazed there I sat,
wishing one day that
He'd reveal to me
Himself so I'd see.

As we prayed that day,
eyes closed the same way,
I, then, was mystified.
I could see His eyes!

Every since that day
often when I pray,
He Shows Me He's There.
I'm grateful He cares.

My Soul Speaks Truth

MAGNIFICENTLY WONDERFUL

When I'm in church on Sunday
or at home on Monday
or driving along the highway on
Tuesday, Wednesday, Thursday, Friday
or any day of the week,
there are precise words I speak
to elicit praises to the Lord.
He
is so worthy of ALL my praise
because of His ever-astonishing ways.
I exalt the Supreme Being in my life
with holy terms -
Hallelujah; I praise you, Father; Thank you, Jesus.
He's always the same.
I glorify His name.

BUT SOMETIMES,
when He so quickly and miraculously
manifests Himself to me,
and I am so wonderfully dazzled
to the utmost degree
by His sometimes
immediate response to me,
I say:'
"HOLY SPIRIT,
YOU ARE JUST SOMETHING ELSE!
WOW! YOU NEVER CEASE TO AMAZE ME!
YOU ARE TOO MUCH!
THANK YOU!
PLEASE KEEP IN TOUCH!

As I utter these words,
I am
almost, always
laughing, giggling, or smiling,
showing great humility, joy and pleasure
BECAUSE of
Who and what He is to me —
He sets me free.
He's Magnificently ....
Wonderful!